Take Me Back to the Tulips

Lin Daniels

Carina,
I hope you enjoy this
poetry collection!
Thankyou,
Lin Daniels

Dedication

To the love of my life, who took me back to the
land of tulips!

.

Contents

Reflections from My Dreams

Starlight creatures wander above me
Whispering mysteries of the Universe
And I lay still, dreaming
Yet, a lot get lost in translation
In my waking hours

The Blues

Rainbows of beauty rejoice
And their tears of joy replenish the Earth
Yet the Earth waddles in a gloom
Over lost colors and wilted flowers
Only feeling the blues!

Paradox

You are the rose, the magic
That I see in this dry desert
A beautiful sight to behold!
Open your eyes,
Even though I'm drifting into slumber

Jasmines are blooming this night
Don't you see them out here?
Your eyes reflecting mirages
Conflicting emotions, that I can't decipher
Is it yearning, revenge, or love?

Tell me who you are
Are you the goddess of love?
Or a pleasant spirit of vengeance?

Tell Us Where You're From

Seven skies above, after passing Milky Way
There lies a kingdom of royal pygmies
Comprising of royal hunters and foragers
A unique group with mystic topaz eyes

Early in the morning, their hunters rise
Chasing their multiple suns, they capture mystic lights
Foragers harvest stardust and space mist
At the end of the day, they exchange stories of adventures

One night, my dream chariot carried me to their land
Passing cosmic wonders, I entered royal Pygymy land
Hearing tales, laughter, and giggles of children
I wished humans could feel the harmony up here

Welcoming me to an intergalactic communion,
I was urged to share stories from the blue-green planet
Should I share greed, cruelty, and pollutions plaguing Earth?
Or of bluest waters and marvelous landscapes?

Tough choice…!

Where Have You been?

When I looked up to the cerulean sky
I saw a star shining so bright
Then it left, waving a bittersweet goodbye
Vanished, gone, dimming its light
But promised to return a time
When dawn arrives, while I waited at twilight

Puzzled, I waited for this moment for long
Losing time, and sometimes hope on the way
Yet we knew our connection was strong,
One of ancient; it held my tears at bay
T'was a "zing," a spark that was always burning
Powerful to unite two hearts in love, across space

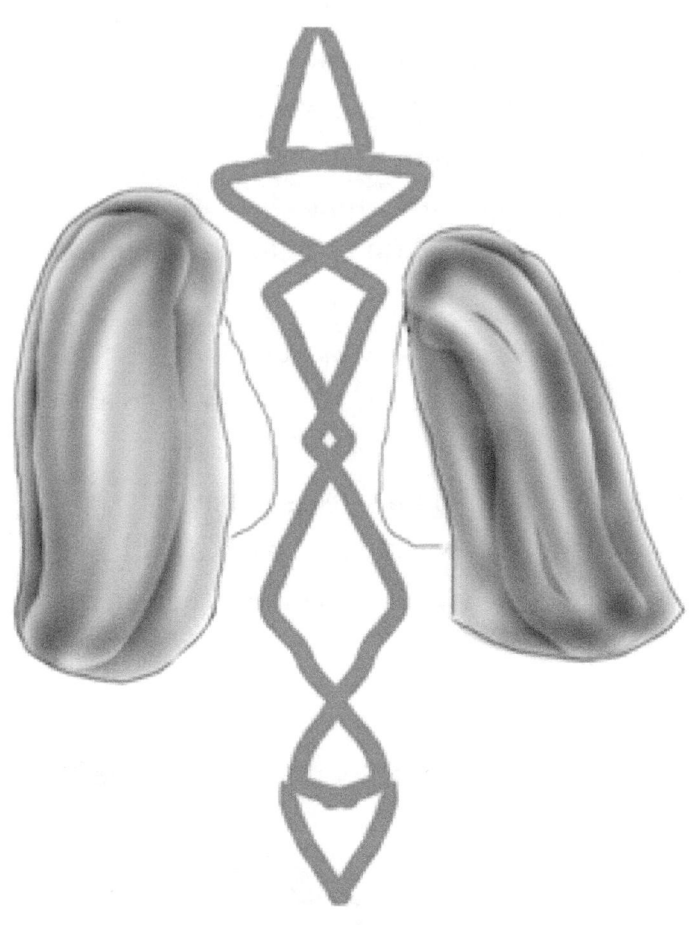

Who Are You?

As I sleep tonight, I see your face
And my face reflected in your eyes
But you close your window to the soul
And I am left pondering the whys, hows, and what-ifs!

Moonlight kisses your cheeks
But you are hiding from it
Living in the shade of gloom, alone
And I wonder, how could this happen!

You are my reflection
My image, my mirror, and self
The paths we walked, ran and skipped
As we thundered down the stairs of joy
The memories, pain, bliss, and loss
How can I forget?
Because I am you!

Moonlit Nights

On certain nights, he arrives
Sometimes with a lullaby,
Sometimes with a flute,
To lull me to sleep

He pulls a cloud blanket over me
Tucks me in among starry hosts
While I twist and turn between midnight folds,
He hums my favorite sleep song

As I fall through galaxies
 I float below vast blue depths
And we fall asleep together
On certain moonlit nights

A Universe of our Own

Your love is so raw
So fresh, so precious
Distance is dwarfed by it
Yet a clear reminder of how far away we are
Even with our hearts so close together

Every hug, kiss, and cuddle are as sweet
As it is painful not to be a reality
As we go through these current times
You there, me here, our love everywhere
Engulfing both of us into a universe of our own!

Mystery Man

Whoever you are, mystery man,
Come into the light so I can see you
If you hide behind the shadows of my dreams
You may only find utter darkness at sunset!

When you give me hopes of a new dawn
I sleep again to reminisce the same
Hoping you'll wait for me at the harbor
As I slowly lull into the stillness of time

At least tell me your name
And I'll stop searching for you
For there are countless faces out there
But none resembles yours...*yet!*

Lotus Bird

Expectations
They crush you, strangle you
Push you to reach up to the sky
Yet grounded to your roots
Why?
I want to break free
And fly high
Like a lotus bird!

Shattered Dreams of Past

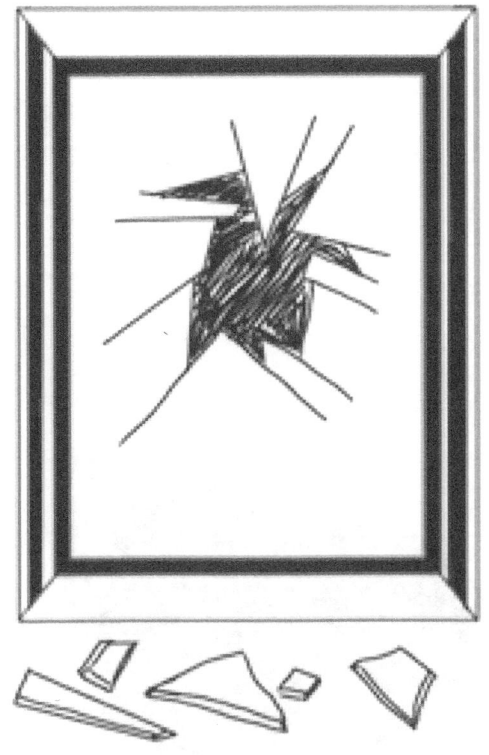

Never look at a broken mirror - they said
I obeyed
They do not know
I am a one with multiple broken pieces

Bleeding in Red

I didn't know you turned my heart so black
When you left
But I was still
Bleeding in red

Broken Pieces

You consumed me whole
But I'm left into pieces, shards, broken
Still reflecting the light left in me
Sparks and waves continue to create
I'll hold on to them for now
Till I return them on the day we'll meet
…someday!

Blank

When you hold a blank slate
A blank canvas
A book with blank pages
Ever get a feeling of new beginnings?
Of starting over?

But that's not what I felt
When I hugged myself
A blank human shell
Empty

Alien

That feeling of losing yourself in someone else
And then you get back to yourself,
You feel alien in your skin

Infested

My thoughts are invaded by pests
Sent by your invisible presence
Parasites that invade private moments
Taking over their host,
Infesting my mind
Alas! My bugged self
Is also the only exterminator present!

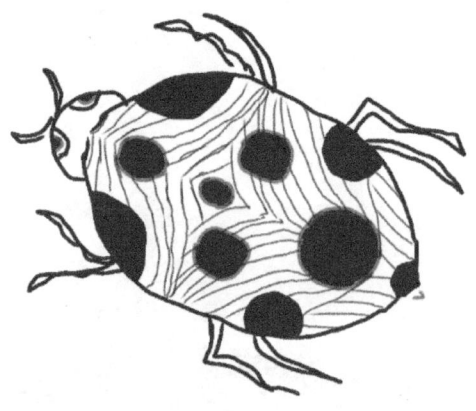

Flashback

Walking a bridge of loneliness
Was my evening routine
An exercise I committed myself to
And eating a soup of salty tears
Was my diet plan

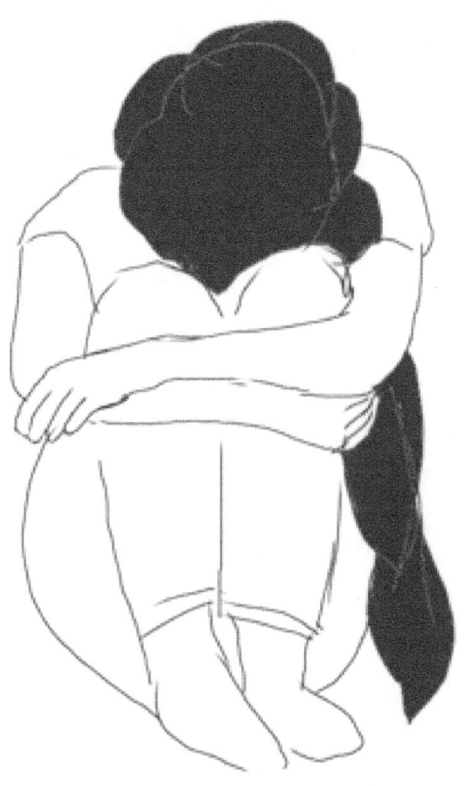

Observations

As I walk through my garden
I overhear a conversation
Ladybug tells a blade of grass
Do not stand so tall
Stoop lower to the ground

Grass:
"I am different than you are, lady
You're all curvy and round
You may not stand tall or fly high
But reserved and slow
Dash of color now, but gone next season"

Ladybug:
"As a lady, I do not condone belittling
If you stopped your pride from growing taller
You would realize the truth
For another blade is around the corner"

Thoughts

Her silence was the loudest scream he had ever heard
But he couldn't bring himself to ask
what happened
He let her be
She always looked down
Spent all her time cocooned in thoughts
Not of her own

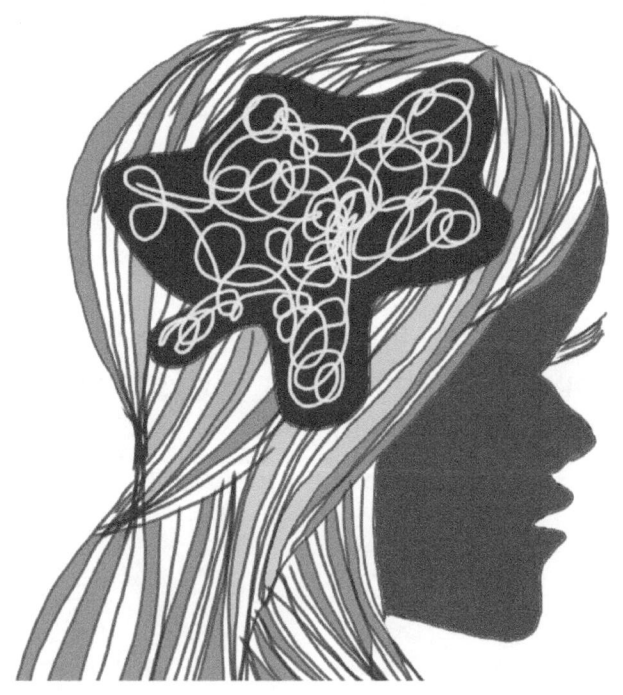

Perspective

Roses were always mute
In his garden
He invited blind bees,
Who kept coming back
Sometimes I wonder
Was I a rose?
Or a bee?

My Friend's Wedding

We met in the Chemistry lab
She shared my name
With her highlighted curls framing her face
She was a true beauty, inside and out

One day I saw her by the stairs
Leaning on a bench, looking forlorn
"I am getting married next month
Everything's all set, perfect, and arranged"

I was at a loss for words
What do I say to her?
"It's okay, I am strong," she said

I saw her next, half a decade later
Her smile was brighter than before
Her rogue curl still danced to the wind

Contradictions

Go away
Hug me tight
Come back
Do not break me again
I forgive you
My heart has yet to

Companion

Leafy years fell
She found her voice, found herself
He was her shadow, her constant
He was there when she took baby steps
He also hoped to be there for her baby's steps, one day
That moody, somber girl was gone
Instead, he saw a confidant young woman
Who loved him, all four legs and furry soul
Her beagle boy, her constant companion

Rehab for Growth

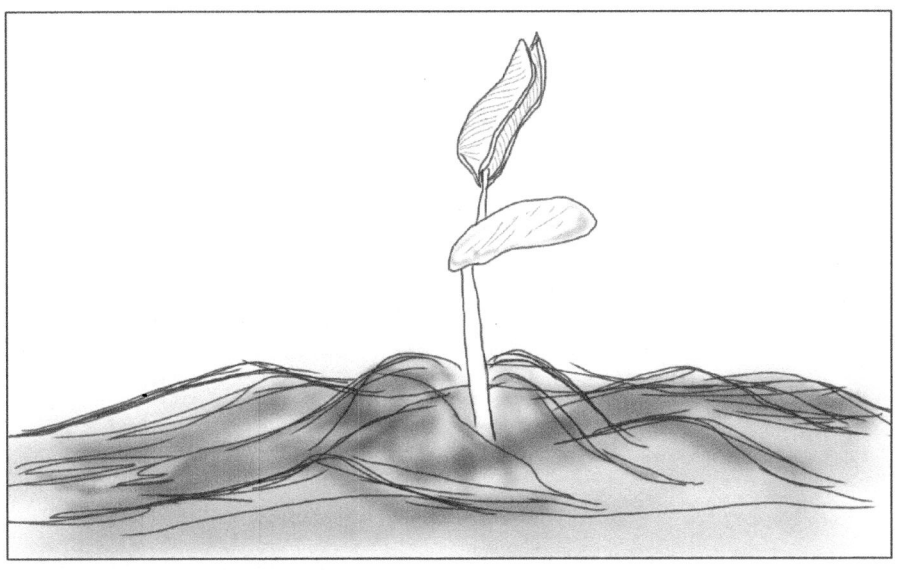

There's always a period of time
A time where you outlive the pain
Endure life and its 'affects'
To dream again, grow, and bloom

Moving forward

Let's not go back to the realm of pain
Let's look up to the pristine skies
Let's celebrate, splashing the rain
Let's cuddle in comfort, closing your eyes!

I Too, was Blind

Don't you know child?
Love is blind

No, I was blind
I realized it too late

My blind heart suffered too
Only because it was stubborn
To open my inner eye
Thus, I wallowed in a darkness
Created and customized for me

Now I see
For I have learned
To never close my inner eye again!

For You

Blossom, for you
Spread fragrance, for you
Be elegant, for you
Shine, for you
Be you, for you
Love, for you

...you've never known!

Away from the misty morning
Toward the wintry sunshine
I see you spread your wings
And flatter up to the teal blue skies
Yes, you're leaving your old nest
In search of heights, you've never known!

Gone is the era of mourning
And of gloomy winds and smog
Yet, the lark still sings
An old sorrowful tune, which you've forgotten
Rise, conquer distances to your East and West
In search of limits, you've never known!

Afar, the wheel of time is turning
Fragrances around here remind me of you
But those are also fading away
Slowly, the memory will be lost
The lyrics will be off rhythm, erased
In search of a song, you've never known!

Lost in flames of a fire, still burning
Contain the nights of mystic dreams, never dreamt
Darkness if hugged by a glowing array,
Of dawn's celestial luster, hope's ignition
Then you will tilt your head, amazed
In search of a beauty, you've never known!

Attachment

Rain kisses me
Showering me with love
Wish I could be free
But I am rooted
Planted here for a purpose
Watch me conquer this mountain
For my roots are strong
I'll wait for a new season of life
And bud, after my rebirth

Self

Escaping reality
Embracing the vast
Inhaling the scent of the air
Being one with my soul

A quivering voice
A lazy brush stroke
A forgotten song lyric
I was all of it, long ago

My words, my story
Nothing will drown my fire
I am no longer enslaved
I broke free of pain's chains

I shall be reborn

Transforming into something unknown
Is this death?
Or reincarnation?

Little Secret

What did Spring tell the cherry blossoms?
"This is your season
-   Bloom!"

Guardian Angel

She came to me one cool afternoon
Tranquility colored her path
Magic helped her move flawlessly
Refractions scattered around her majestic aura

She fanned her exquisite wings
Her gaze with those soulful eyes left me speechless
"I am a messenger," she says
"Sent by the souls high above, watching over us"

I think back to those fairy movies
Disney's taught me all I need to know
But this is different, too ethereal
Her presence demanded attention

"Time to let go of your heartache"

Tulips Blooming

It started with a dark rose
Hold on to it
How can I?
When my love lives among tulips

I knew I was ready to bloom again

Love Finds a Way

Seeking an answer
While not fully knowing the question
That's how it feels to search for love
Do not search for it, my dears
Let love find you on its own
Destiny will bring love to you
And when it happens,
It will be a match made in heaven!

If It's Meant to Be

I was a character in a love story
Written in pages of the cosmos
Force of the universe whispered to the story:
If it's meant to be, you'll receive glory

Seasons passed, eons fell
Galaxies hid their faces from darkness
My character went in search of peace
If it's meant to be, all resistance will cease

Gods of mythology gathered around
Saturn and Venus looked on me with favor
"Will love find her, or will it look for another?
If it's meant to be, they will find each other"

The love story's hero appeared on its pages
He was dormant, asleep in space frost
He was looking for his soulmate, his love
If it's meant to be, she'll be one with the eyes of a dove

When stars aligned one misty morning
They crossed paths and felt a spark
They looked back, noticing their missing half
If it's meant to be, they'll look back to this day and laugh

These are not star-crossed lovers
They came from unknown origins, crossed hurdles
Their love filled with emotions, stories, and light
If it's meant to be, you'll realize glory comes after night

Soulmate

Our souls met in some previous birth,
In an age of innocence
We made pinky promises to each other
Come find me in the next birth

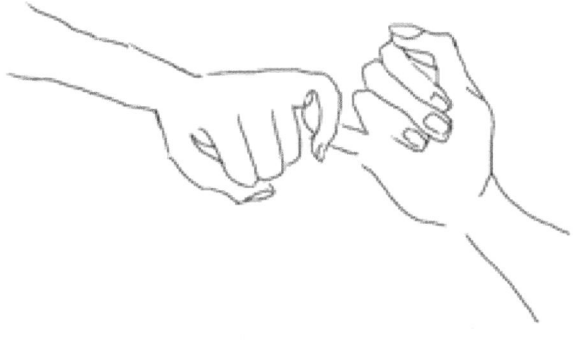

We Speak the Same Language

I walk into the coffee shop
There's a calming aura here, people are scarce
I place my order, scan the shop
For a comfy corner
To cozy up to this vibe

And there I find him
A grown man, reading poetry
I recognize the title
It's about life, love, and rebirth
I understand it

Once upon a time,
I was intimate with its delicate pages
It helped me heal – heart, mind, and soul
While I was in a deep, dark space
While I was trying to escape life's maze

I walk forward with courage
"Hi" – I say to the reader!

This is my blooming phase
I reassured myself

Trust

"Close your eyes"
He whispered
"Why?" I asked
"I want to show you a world of dreams –
Our dreams
…will you let me?"
As I closed my eyes, he knew my answer
And he closed his eyes too

56

Take Me Back to the Tulips

Take me back to the tulips
Where my dreams bloom
Take me back to hear gallops
Where sunshine rids day's gloom
Away from a starry night,
Right into the blinding light,
Take me back to that happy place
Take me back to nature's sweetest embrace!

Take me back to dawn's luster
Where my wings unfold to fly
Take me back to that jasmine cluster
Where my soul leaps up to the sky
Away from mystic symphonies of night,
Right into glistening waves of light,
Take me back to that dove's nest
Take me back to affection's best!

Take me back to the seashore
Where my hope awakens slowly
Take me back to the snow and more
Where my reality delights wholly
Away from twilight or night,
Right into the radiant light,
Take me back to where kites glide
Take me back to where hearts collide!

Somewhere, somehow…

Early morning dew reminds me of you
And I wish I was there with you
Evening mist when you take a walk
Makes me wish you were here to talk
Wishes here, wishes there…
Somewhere, somehow, our wishes are everywhere!

Auroral lights gleam above, so far away
I wish you could see them a while and stay
Thunderbolts roar among afternoon rains
Makes me wish we were in summer plains
Wishes glow, wishes grow…
Somewhere, somehow our wishes flow!

Be radiant as you are, my velvet sunset
I'll promise to be your sunrise blanket
To sleep and rise, knowing this bliss
To dream and fly, we will never miss
Wishes shine, wishes divine…
Somewhere, somehow, our wishes entwine!

Confirmed with a Kiss

Daunting dreams of the future took hold of my mind
Meaningless memories of the past loomed atop my head
No…not this time,
This is my second chance
"Are you sure?" - they asked
"I choose him"
Just like he chose me
Opening my eyes, I felt peace
No nightmares, no memories with tear stains
I am wrapped safely in his arms
Placing a sweet kiss on my lips, he confirmed
His choice – Me!
He did not need any words for it,
And I reciprocated

Mood Swings

While wallowing in a pit of my creation
I was given a ladder
Why?
"Cause you need to come out of there"
But I like it here, for now
"You need to come up and see the world"
I once trusted that world blindly
"Your tulips have blossomed into their fullness"
Yes, I planted them a long time ago,
Eons ago, a time before my heartache
They must be beautiful now -
"We can see it together if you let me"
I would love that!
And I climbed up

Tulip-less Bouquet

Once upon a time,
I was among the crowd of eligible bachelorettes
Hoping I would not catch the bridal luck
To become 'next' down the aisle
Only because I wasn't ready

But I caught it, stunned, while everyone cheered
I was a single woman
Not committed to settling

Years passed; others got married
I still held on to that one bouquet I caught
I was determined to wait for my beast

One day, I found him in a castle of tulips

My Stories

Trapped in a fog of fantasy
Nourished by colors of myth,
Infinite stories cried out,
"Let us out,
We'll take you on a magical tour
And teach you of spells' allure!"

Blooming Dreams

You know your dreams are blooming
When your reality becomes what you once dreamed
You know your joy is looming
When your gratitude makes you self-content

Now, look up to the midnight sky
And relax by the sand

Midnight Leaves

They fly by close to midnight
Whispering tales of their journey

Once, they crossed the seven seas
After swimming in the fountain of youth
They know not its coordinates
When I asked them where it is

They come by my window every fall
And tell me the world is changing colors again
I tell them it's a pattern
You should know, for you are leaves

They tell me I am wrong,
For to them, they are much more than that
And when midnight left, they flew with it to the horizon!

Rebirth

Innocent and pure
She bloomed in life
Only to receive a grief
She wilted, fell to the ground
Faded in time

The fertile ground gave her a second chance
Her roots helped her rise
To uplift those around
To bloom again, this time for her
This is rebirth!

Lioness

Past:
I am a seed
Flying in an endless sky
Reality brings me crashing down
I am thrown away like a weed

Present
I draw my energy from the Sun
I extend my petals till the Moon
As I flaunt my magnificent mane
Yes, I am a lioness now!

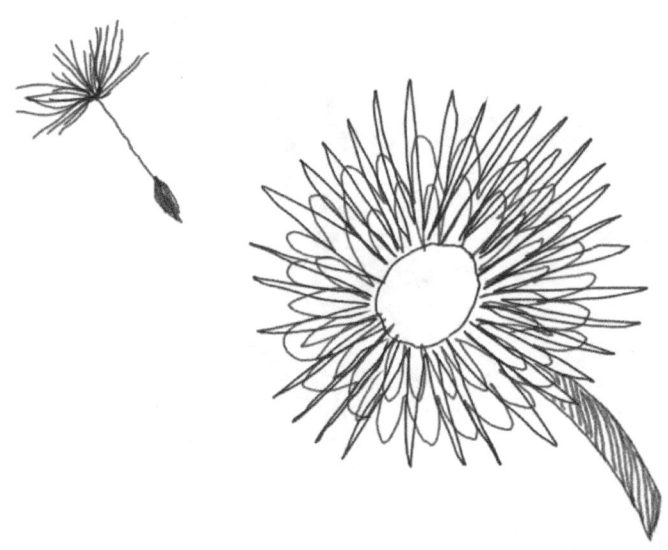

Closure

Chin up, head held high
Thriving in life
Eyes wide open, ears on alert
Glowing as a wife

This is to all of them
Who tried to bring me down
This is to take pride in
All my achievements – my shining crown

All the taunts, glares, words with knives
With them, you tried to take away my light
I forgive you for your actions
You did not know what you were doing

Queen of Blossoms

Gliding up to face me
She stopped, fluttered her wings
Reflecting her maker's craft
Commanding attention to the tune she sings

Tapestry set alive in her wings
They tell a story of creation
Mesmerizing the beholder's eyes
 Filling their mind with elation

"You are blooming" – she says
I smile, nodding my head
"It was high time for a visit
For I wanted to celebrate with you this achievement"

Flowerchild

Following a rebirth and subsequent blooming
She was asked to represent
A highest order of individuals,
Who defeated dormancy, a state of barren life

She created the utopian garden from her dreams
One which only she could see, or to whom she invited
A garden similar to the age-old *Eden*
A heavenly place for her to be in

She was the garden and the gardener
Her nightly escapes from garden
Resulted in time well rested, rejuvenated
Har garden is timeless, spaceless, found only in her reality!

Weaving New Dreams

Spinning silk strands of hopes
Circling a web of dreams
Nature's artist and performer
Fiercely rooted yet hanging by a silk thread
Freely gliding
That's the new me now!

When Love Blossomed

"How did your love blossom?
Tell us your love story!"

And I did:

When I looked for love
I found it all around in elemental forms

I felt loved by the air, water,
Luscious Earth, and cool fire

When love looked for me
It found me under a maple tree

One fine Autumn evening
Love took its human form

And we chatted, all evening
Throughout the night
Into the morning!

My love and I never felt bound by time
We watered our newfound feelings with romance

And it blossomed into something more
Something I cannot find words yet to describe!

Keep Blooming

They will tell you:
You are lacking,
You are weak
You are ugly
You are a failure
You are fearful

You are enough; fulfill your purpose in life
You are strong; you've overcome countless challenges
You are beautiful; their eyes fail to see your elegance
You are successful; your achievements speak for themselves
You are brave; you've mastered your fears

Remember and be who you are
Do not let anyone tell you otherwise
For "they" will tell you many things
They may trample your blooms
They may dry out your self-confidence

Do not let your blooms wilt
Do not let your light fade
Do not let anyone hinder your growth

Eternal Travelers

Let us go to the vineyards
Let us watch the Sunrise
Amidst clouds of morning mist
Let us spend our days in the valley of grapes
Counting our blessings, both past, and future

Let us go to the beach
Let us watch waves that say 'hi'
And those which retreat with 'bye'
Let us spend our days in the honey-golden sand
Wondering at the star-sprinkled sky

Let us go to the woods
Let us watch the green canopy of trees
Standing tall, undisturbed, and somber
Diverse in their color, shade, form, and growth
Let us spend traversing through dense forest
Finding a clearing at the end for us and a picnic

Let us go home
Let us watch how our days begin and nights end here
Where every shade of love blooms and grows
Let us spend time in ignorant bliss
Listening to your heart beating and mine!

Do we truly belong to one place more than others?
Maybe, for our existence is more than a place,
It is a feeling of attachment, an emotion!
You will know when you reach that final destination!

ABOUT THE BOOK:

Take Me Back to the Tulips *is a self-illustrated collection of poems by Lin Daniels, intended for all those who have dreamed and hoped to bloom. Love, loss, personal struggle, heartbreaks, growth, and joy are facets of great magnitude in life. But choosing to bloom despite going through all of life's hurdles indicates inner strength. This book is divided into five sections, each exploring different themes: Reflections from My Dreams, Shattered Dreams of Past, Rehab for Growth, Love Finds a Way, and Blooming Dreams. Together they tell a tale of heartbreak, personal transformation, and love entwined with imagination and creativity.*

ABOUT THE AUTHOR:

Lin Daniels is an artist, tea-enthusiast, and writer, who loves to paint with words and colors. Daniels first started writing poems when she was in middle school as a way of expressing her thoughts and imagination. **Take Me Back to the Tulips** *is her first published collection of poetry, named after the first poem she'd written many years ago, to her one true love! She is now married to him, and together, they continue their traveling adventures. When she is not writing or traveling, she can be found reading historic romance novels at home or writing at the local library. Daniels lives with her husband in Michigan.*

Made in United States
Cleveland, OH
12 November 2025

25831783R00052